# ADVANCE PRAISE FOR DAVID SILVERBERG AND *AS CLOSE TO THE EDGE WITHOUT GOING OVER*

"This book is a time machine. With nostalgia and wit, these poems bring us to childhood shrines of forgotten manuscripts and pop culture, while forecasting the future we may face: a crossroads where each person has to decide what they stand for, and how to make themselves heard. Part celebration, part call-to-action, David Silverberg uses these pages to remind poets and readers alike: we need you now more than ever."

—Alessandra Naccarato, winner of the Writers' Trust RBC Bronwen Wallace Award, and of the 2017 CBC Poetry Prize

"Turning his sweet tooth into a Bluetooth connected to the future, David Silverberg explores a future where a man's brain is one with the internet and where language is changing so fast it's sometimes too gizzle and gronk for us to keep up. I recommend you check out all the other words David has to offer in this new collection."

—RC Weslowski, broadcaster and Canadian poetry slam champion

# As Close To The Edge Without Going Over

## David Silverberg

**FIRST EDITION**
*As Close To The Edge Without Going Over* © 2019 by David Silverberg
Cover art & layout © 2019 by Jared Shapiro

All Rights Reserved.

This book is a work of fiction. Names, characters, places, and incidents are either a product of the author's imagination or are used fictitiously. Any resemblance to actual events, locales, or persons, living or dead, is entirely coincidental.

Distributed in Canada by
Fitzhenry & Whiteside Limited
195 Allstate Parkway
Markham, Ontario L3R 4T8
Phone: (905) 477-9700
e-mail: bookinfo@fitzhenry.ca

Distributed in the U.S. by
Consortium Book Sales & Distribution
34 Thirteenth Avenue, NE, Suite 101
Minneapolis, MN 55413
Phone: (612) 746-2600
e-mail: sales.orders@cbsd.com

**Library and Archives Canada Cataloguing in Publication**

Title: As close to the edge without going over / David Silverberg
Names: Silverberg, David, 1980- author.
Description: Poems.
Identifiers: Canadiana (print) 20190061804 | Canadiana (ebook) 20190061812 | ISBN 9781771484848
  (softcover) | ISBN 9781771484855 (PDF)
Classification: LCC PS8637.I359 A82 2019 | DDC C811/.6—dc23

KQP
an imprint of ChiZine Publications
Peterborough, Canada
www.chizinepub.com
info@chizinepub.com

Edited by Sandra Kasturi

 Canada Council   Conseil des arts
for the Arts     du Canada

We acknowledge the support of the Canada Council for the Arts which last year invested $20.1 million in writing and publishing throughout Canada.

Published with the generous assistance of the Ontario Arts Council.

Printed in Canada

# As Close To The Edge Without Going Over

poems

David Silverberg

KQP
an imprint of ChiZine Publications

## Contents

| | |
|---|---|
| Burn | 9 |
| Download | 10 |
| Groove | 12 |
| Terms and Conditionals | 13 |
| They Come for Our Words | 16 |
| Given the Chance | 18 |
| Windows | 20 |
| Butterscotch | 21 |
| New World Aphorisms | 22 |
| Upon Learning Doug Ford Will Be Ontario's Next Premier | 23 |
| The Jealous Eye | 24 |
| I'm Not Like the Other Guys Because My Brain Is Fused to the Internet | 26 |
| Transdifferentiation | 29 |
| YouTube Hole | 30 |
| Come Back | 31 |
| Fuck You, OCD | 32 |
| Unsolicited | 33 |
| Precious | 34 |
| Short Forms | 37 |
| Exhibit | 38 |
| People to Avoid | 39 |
| 'Til It's Gone | 40 |
| Unfold | 42 |
| Mall Rats | 43 |
| Nature Algorithms | 45 |
| Famous Works of Literature that Also Describe the Night I Made Out with My First Alien | 46 |
| The Ghosts that Love Me | 47 |
| For Emily | 49 |
| Bookmobile | 51 |
| Sense-ual | 54 |

| | |
|---|---:|
| Listicle | 55 |
| Give Me | 56 |
| The Gun | 57 |
| For My Mother | 59 |
| Villains | 62 |
| Today Is OK | 65 |
| When They Killed the Journalists | 66 |
| When We Die | 67 |
| The End of It All | 68 |
| | |
| Acknowledgements | 71 |
| About the Author | 72 |

# Burn

When the world burned
we were kissing each other's clavicles.

It came fast and heavy,
like the tornado of fire.

We closed our eyes and let the heat shudder over our curled bodies.

It was the closest we'd been for seven months.

And we stayed that way,
long after the rubble was excavated
long after the sifters tasted the last grumble of dirt.

Our bones became trophies of raised-fist triumph,
your hands still on my hips.

## Download

When we began to download our dreams
they were traded from phone to phone
like mint-condition Fleer baseball cards.

I'll give you my nightmare
for your lucid dream.

Some of us just wanted to offload
fertile images
of shattered glass, megaphone shouts,
fingernails pressed into palms.
Others had to taste a slice of horror
when their dreams wafted with
frilly filters
and lavender perfume.

We weren't prepared for the hurricanes
of downloads
overheating the app's servers
cutting the umbilical sensor linking
our subconscious
to the app's mainframe.
All those dreams now pouring
out of the Cloud
drenching the flailing ground
with the fears,
regrets
REM therapy
cartoon caricatures.
What we couldn't predict,
what no one could floorplan
was how the bug spray of these
unclaimed dreams
took on their own heartbeat, sentient as soon as we discarded them.

The dreams enlightened themselves,
but also defended their existence with
the violence of a mother harbouring her young.

To watch willed dreams
manifest themselves into reality,
away from our fluttering eyelids that used to spring open,
wash the dream clean from our brain's shadows.

These new monsters splintered our resolve.
So we ran from our dreams.
Like we hadn't been taught to do.
We ceded authority to wisps
of ephemera you never thought
would stomp firm on the earth.
Our stomachs clenched.
We realized we had no choice but one.
This was war.

## Groove

And a one, two, one, two, three, four
and we slip into that electric latitude

skin and beer breath holding hands under strobe lights
flicking away yesterday's bullet points
like crumbs off a collar

our fingers splaying into jazz notes
the bass scarfing our throats
it's all such a beautiful buffet

we need this
we want this

punching clocks isn't as cathartic
as we thought it'd be
The clocks self-repair within seconds
We shake our heads at the inanity of it all
then shake what our mama gave us

we are geeks of nature abandoning our routine
to recess under trembling beats
hungry to fuse rhythm onto our bones

someone starts to breakdance
someone shouts "Give no fucks!"
fist-bumps canopy the dance circle

this sweat is the lubricant of the congregation
and we moonwalk until the sun yawns awake
it's what we do now. It's what we should've done a long time ago.

# Terms and Conditionals

Thanks for purchasing the latest Augmented Phone!

You can acquire Content on our Services for free or for a charge, which will come as a form of a credit-card payment or a drop of your mitochondrial DNA.

Each Transaction is an electronic contract between you and Zaphex, but we are under no obligation to meet your parents and/or play nice with your cousins. However, if you are a customer of Zaphex Distribution International and you acquire an App or a book, our Distribution team may send a representative to taste that new pasta primavera you cooked up Sunday night, yet we are under no obligation to Instagram it.

When you make your first Transaction or DNA droplet, we will ask you to choose how frequently we should ask for your password for future purchases. Your password should be a minimum of seven characters and have some, well, character, and include at least an Aramaic letter, half a pun and a melody from a Nina Simone song.

If you enable Emotion ID for Transactions, we will ask you to authenticate all Transactions with your BrainPrint and sense of humour. Failure to make our machine-learning program even chuckle may result in the failure to confirm said Transaction.

All Transactions are final, unless you can prove you were delightfully drunk and/or self-loathing at the moment of purchase. A Zaphex ID employee may visit your home to root through your recycling to check for empty booze bottles, or scavenge your bedroom floor for Lay's bags.

Content prices may change at any time, especially on our bad days, like when one of our Chinese manufacturers reports of another suicide attempt by $3/hour workers.

If technical problems prevent or unreasonably delay delivery of Content, your exclusive and painfully sole remedy is either replacement of the Content or mixing the blood of a grumpy escape-room operator with the moustache grease of a Russian hacker. We will accept North Korean hacker moustache grease if a Russian hacker cannot be sourced in time.

Using our Services and accessing your Content requires a Zaphex ID, and being acutely aware of how cool our company has become in the past decade. A Zaphex ID is the account you use across our Neurosystem, including astral planes where variations of our Company may exist. Your Zaphex ID is valuable, and you are responsible for maintaining its confidentiality and security. Don't tell it to this new girl you're dating, we really don't think it's going to last beyond six weeks. And definitely don't use it as your safe word.

Zaphex is not responsible for any losses or sudden depression arising from the unauthorized use of your Zaphex ID. Please contact Zaphex if you suspect that your Zaphex ID has been compromised. The surest method of contacting us is screaming into your pillow for 10 minutes, or shaking your fists to the heavens like an old-timey curmudgeon.

You may use the Services and Content only for personal, noncommercial purposes, and it's encouraged to promote our Content to nearby Samsung users and report back to Zaphex Distribution International the degree of jealousy you detect in their eyes, cheeks and dry elbow skin.

Zaphex's delivery of Content does not transfer any promotional use rights to you, even if you really really like that Tetris game that's not really Tetris but is revamped for the modern era with slicker graphics.

You can use Content from up to five different Zaphex IDs on each device. We may also augment your boring life from up to 25 different devices.

It is your responsibility not to lose, destroy, or make naughty with Content once downloaded. We encourage you to back up your Content regularly, and when doing so you are required to evoke a truck-backing-up noise. Yes, we will be listening.

You may not tamper with or circumvent any security technology included with the Services. Doing so may result in the ghost of faulty microprocessors haunting your Saturday afternoon naps.

We may amend these Terms and Conditions at any time by posting the amended terms on our Instagram profile. Please ignore the manicured cheerleading photos of our "engaging workplace culture" populating that feed at any given moment. Our right to amend the Conditions includes the right to modify, add to, or pointlessly reduce the font size of said terms in the document. We will provide you 30.75 days' notice by posting the amended terms.

# They Come for Our Words

The demons have come, but we didn't think they'd come for
our tongues first.
Not the flappy crepe waggling between our lips.
They have come for our language.
Somehow, somewhy some of us can't say the words
thundering in our throats.
They become a puddle, a scab wound, a teenager
fumbling for a bra clasp,
and so we can't organize like we normally could have.
The demons,
they know how to separate the strong from the meek,
some of us become appetizers for their sword-sized fangs.
I'm hoping to spoil their dinner.

See, I'm writing all this down
before they can steal my written words.
I hear it's been happening all over the world.
My tongue, they have, and they've forked it
like their own gruesome gods,
but I know how they do what they brew,
because I heard their mud voices on the way to get rations,
they can be real sloppy when they're
feeding on our children.
They didn't notice my ears pressed against those
blood-drenched doors
and they don't knizslock how we infilcrampled
that meeting where their hushed tones
built into a fevered pitch of mad wimpledander

Oh no. It's happening isn't it?

DAVID SILVERBERG

OK, let me spew this out like it's a black licorice Slurpee.
They start with our langfandango
and jimble down to our ears, an infection that trimpsies into
every way we have to communi-skate.
We soon go deaf. It's a slow burfle.
And it's making us go mad.
Which is exactly what those cantapoles want.

Oh god, it's getting worse isn't it?

My hands aren't quisping what I want to orqua
my eyes are feeling drevvy with yurgur
and every time I want to olbert to you
what I need to asperf, it all comes out
psychofriscooalphametabioaquadoloop.

The demons are planning to stromponi the entire luminaria!
Fleeze hurkle me!
My name is Cruttlemask CasketSlape and I live at
Tangerdream Examper in St. Crusky and and—

Oh. It's too late isn't it?

## Given the Chance

She said I could live forever
just this pill
this regimen
it was experimental
as these trials tend to be
but what did I have to lose?

At 85, not much,
maybe my favourite seat at
the retirement centre dining room
the odd furtive glance from Sonia in 18B.

I took the pill
and others like it.
I washed it down with shandies,
just how my father took his Lipitor pills
back in the 2020s.

Now,
I don't like how my skin looks on my bones,
shiny,
elastic
like overcompensating CGI.

Now,
I'm more alone than ever
not just because my friends have left
but I don't know how to speak to anyone.
Everyone is all Facebook Glasses
drone warfare
food capsules.
I hate to sound cranky
so I won't.
Sound, that is.

| DAVID SILVERBERG

I prefer silence over the whir of whining.
No one forced my hand
to grip the azure pill,
throw it back into my throat,
feel its cell-regeneration powers
shiver through my body.
It wasn't supposed to be like this.
I could've said no.
I could've died like you all did,
and now I'm a vampire in gridlock,
unable to fly
or peek outside the labyrinth walls.

# Windows

As an optometrist,
Miles always knew there was a quote
shaking with such bullseye truth
he kept its secret boxed into his chest.

"The eyes are the windows to the soul."

Yes. They are. Miles has endured it, first-hand
when he first laid his hands on the ophthalmoscope
and peered into Lucy's eyes, as she complained
of intense ocular pressure.

He saw something he shouldn't. A hacker's source code
dozens of driver's licenses.
How was this possible? He swallowed his question,
told Lucy she was OK, swore to himself for daydreaming at work
but then, patient after patient, he saw the same thing.

Well, never the same filmic scenes, always a fresh collage
of men, women and even children baring their lies and loves
when their eyelids parted the curtain to let him in.

He was a bystander to their affairs,
murders,
grinning wins,
bubbling ambitions,
all dilated with an energy that Miles could practically
hear as velvet whispers murmur,
"Look at us. We're not afraid of who we are."

Miles never turned away from their eyes.
He couldn't help it. And he couldn't help them
because, one day, he pressed his eyes to the mirror
finally
and saw the buried bones he had long been hiding behind his retinas.

# Butterscotch

Do you remember how tall we felt when we scampered on top of the toboggan hill & we tumbled into the tree to earn a broken arm and yearbook signatures on the cast & how we swam at Wasaga with three beers glowing in our chest & how we skipped from Wonderland rollercoaster to funnel-cake regrets to drooping ride home & how we built a crowd from the detritus of a 4am Nuit Blanche to cypher poetry at Trinity Bellwoods & the drive to Huntsville singing Blues Traveller & that time Raine Maida came to the poetry slam and showed off Chantal's pregnant belly & what the boom of the bass felt like when dancing trumpeted in our sternum & those Jell-O shooters turning that Canada Day into a messy karaoke party & comics we kept (unwittingly) from our days bouncing into Bookmobiles & the cigarettes you bummed from Amanda & the rum balls you bought from Steeles Bakery & the laughter that gurgled from your dad's throat & the eyes pivoting to the ground from girlfriends who didn't know what to say, what needed to be said, what you wanted to say too & the Twitter notifications distracting you from writing haikus & the hopscotch you played when dog owners on your street were callously careless & how you tasted butterscotch whenever you thought of your grandparents & how you still can't do a Jumble without thinking of Bubbie & the first time Emily's baby hands gripped my finger & the stories printed and bound & that shimmered with a solemn peace rarely found since & how it used to be?

# New World Aphorisms

The early bird catches the software worm.

Let sleeping blogs lie.

Ain't no party like a cosplay party!

Geek and destroy.

All spellcheck's broken loose!

Nerd-sightedness is the ability to see value beyond what is in one's own inner circle.

You're only good as your last tweet.

Have I captcha'd your attention?

## Upon Learning Doug Ford Will Be Ontario's Next Premier

Hey, poets.
It's time to get to work.

# The Jealous Eye

*Inspired by the story of Ron Spence, a Canadian man who lost his right eye as a child and when he was older he placed a special camera in his eye socket to record footage of what he saw.*

I can feel you smile.
Eyes can't smile,
but your crow's feet are stretching their fingers again.
I can practically hear your morning giggles.

He's decided to camera you hasn't he?

You're such a sad socket. You really can't see what he's doing.

This schtick is just for kicks.
You'll be the circus ringleader for 30 seconds, tops.
Then your red light will dim,
the applause will coddle you no longer,
he'll be shaking hands
and patching you up,
hiding you from awkward glances,
stumbling fingers.

He even called himself a freak.
*Let's put the one-eyed camera-face on stage again,
Dance for us, cyborg, dance!*

At least I have vision for the future.
He NEEDS me.

You're just a bucket where all the coins beach
waiting to be plucked, to funeral his eyelids,
        that long riverboat tour soundtracked by bagpipes.

You probably didn't even know he's Scottish, did you?

| DAVID SILVERBERG

Jesus.

All you do is
Show up!
Spread your eyelids
Get to makeup!
Wardrobe.
On in 5!

You don't know what I see.

You don't shiver when tears maze down his face.

You don't hear kids bleating like pirates,
as if I never went to high school with daggers and nunchuks.

Maybe it's better that way. That just one of us looks out into the abyss.
    It can be dewy grass and flirting rainbows one second,
        then a woman flinging her feces at a Tim Horton's cashier. Yes,
        that happened.

I hate you. But you're my brother. My friend. The only
one who understands my chaotic corneas.

You still light a fire under the blood of many.
    You give hope to cyborgs who want to see
more than just an Eyeborg.

I might see the world, but you can make it better.

## I'm Not Like the Other Guys Because My Brain Is Fused to the Internet

In high school
I blended into the background like
manila envelopes at a post office.
No one noticed me.
I was OK with that.
But when the Neurolennium Project came to our school,
asking for volunteers for a new program,
my hand shot up higher than everyone else's.
It helped I was jumping.

I love experiments. I made
necklaces that could detect heartburn
before it struck.
My mom threw them out though,
wishing I focused more on my homework
than building biomedical devices.

When the Project leaders told me they could
bind my brain waves to the Internet,
(and I mean the ENTIRE Internet)
I thought I was on some half-baked TV show
where a C-list celeb-show host
would jump into the room
scream "Gotcha!" and the set would fizzle away to reveal
a rabidly enthralled audience.

But they were serious. I was deadpan too.
Yes, I said. I want this.
I need to see what this would do to me.

The operation felt like
swimming in jelly.
My fingers could grasp the air,
my eyes stung,
and when I woke up,
the doctors said I could simply flip a switch on my hip.
Great, now I have a weird hip goiter-switch.
Whatever. Doesn't matter. This was too good to pass up.

I'm not like the other guys.
I can access the RottenTomato score
of that movie we should see.
Top Critic reviews? I got you!

We can trail our fingers along the
spine of Airbnb,
thinking aloud
where this touch will take us.

I go to the Dark Web too.
They couldn't filter it out from the surgery.
I know way too much about
cellars of blood money
destined to disappear behind Bitcoin wires.
So I might be moody sometimes,
no more than the average guy, maybe.
But do you think you could love a man
whose emotions are tethered to the
rocketing code tick-tocking
in his cells?

I know this may be too much,
      like how my motoring mouth
can smash a bucket of words into the air.
So if you can excuse the odd pop-up tic
and take me for who I am,
you could be the wife of the first
guy with his brain fused to the Internet.
Don't you like the wedding ring of that?

# Transdifferentiation

A specific species of jellyfish
found off the coast of Japan
looks no different than a tiny hairy thimble
floating serene in the ocean.
This fish has a sterling reason to be
grinning fin to fin.
It's known as the immortal jellyfish
because it can reverse the aging process,
reconstituting itself as a juvenile—
as if a butterfly could flutter back in time
to become a caterpillar once again.

I begin to cuddle close to this idea.

I wonder what it'd be like
to feel the grey hairs shade back into brown
the ankle pain to exit-stage left,
banished from the stage for now.
Would all that makes me what I am
take a bold lunge back in time,
when I was learning to braid ambition into passion?

I have too many questions, not enough answers,
especially for this magic sequestered far from my species.

What I do know is that I wonder and wander
more than I hunger for that cycle of
caterpillar chronology.
It could be a curse in disguise if I revert to
the juvenile version
of the adult I've tried to carve from raw clay.
And it may ring like a cliché, but I'm happy with who I am,
the wrinkles under my bad decisions,
the halos around the summits I've flag-planted.
Anything else would feel like
I'm cheating in a game I've agreed
to play, by the rules established before I was even a flicker
on the earth's axis.

## YouTube Hole

I'm sunk.

Caught between Larry David interviews
Carpool Karaoke with the Chili Peppers.
Damn, YouTube must know I love Flea.

I juke left, stiff-arm the "subscribe now" claw,
get to the lip of this sandtrap,
hug my chin over the edge, come on,
hoist into a Monty Python skit with its sepia slapstick.

Yes. *Phew.*
The cheese shop.
Genius at its most dairy.

I don't need to curb my enthusiasm
Or give it away now.
I got the YouTube hole I wanted
this silly salad of wordplaygrounds,
rubber bumper legs.

I'm home.

## Come Back

The night tastes iron.

Cradling your head,
    I tell you I love you.
You go somewhere just then
    eyes scattering to the ceiling,
then turning away quick from the jagged lights,
the bright that always made you squint

The Ultra SSRIs have taken you from me,
from us,
as if your voice was stolen from your throat.

You're supposed to smile at Corrie character twists,
dirty jokes from that old book of limericks,
supposed to dig your fingernails into palms at the
newscast when the anchor pronounces Notre Dame "like such an
American."

I look out the window, at the wrinkled overcoats
mumbling their shuffles across the outstretched garden.

You're somewhere. Far from me, holding your still limbs,
my fingers brushing the sleep that never seems to leave
your eye corners.

I want to break the serious fog hanging over us.
We haven't laughed in a long time. We did.
Back in the day. Before the sickness assaulted
the heat that hung lantern in your chest.

This is a dream I want you to wake from.
And so I sing you whimsy
your favourite Gilbert & Sullivan melodies
hoping it lifts the heavy blanket
pressing you against this sunken bed.

# Fuck You, OCD

You mangler of thought

You gaping thunderstorm

You cleaver of memories

You acid-tipped poison dart

You mystery lunch meat

You tongue sore refusing to heal

You sickly buffet soaked in bile

You ashtray messy with tics

You unflushed toilet

You screaming silence

You ringtone of scimitars

You heartburn recipe, like mixing wine with milk

You house of unholy

You kidnapper of fathers.

# Unsolicited

Today
men no longer send unsolicited photos
of their dicks
in all their monstrous disgrace.

Instead
women receive
unsolicited cellphone pics
of bookshelves.

"This is what I'm reading, you into Sedaris?"
reads a common dating-profile caption.

Women no longer cringe
from genitalia warfare
but they swipe left fast
when they see shelves
of high-school textbooks hugging dust,
only the required reading lazing in the screenshot.

It's a deeper rejection.
She wonders:
*What kind of man doesn't read?!*

Now men go desperate on Craigslist
begging for strangers to fill their
shelves,
buying yellowed books to
display their faux passion.
A premium is placed on libraries of
Vonnegut, Didion, Roxane Gay.
Look at that range!

# Precious

### I.

My mom doesn't want to me to leave this house.
She thinks the New World will kill me, somehow.
But I tell her about Joey and Lindsay and Raman and
how their parents let them play in the Guarded Zone.
Their faces are streamers and birthday cake
and grass-stained knees.

But she shakes her tired head.
Tells me to stay indoors, always,
I'm not like the others,
I'm more . . . precious.
She always pauses before saying "precious"
as if she's trying to coil the word around her tongue before
she ends up saying it anyway.

Halloween this year,
I'm going with Joey to trick 'n' speak.
It's time to be an outlaw. For once.
These walls, this clogged air, this routine,
it's all so expected and I can't live like an animal boxed into a corner.

### II.

I'm sent to bed at 8,
as always,
but tonight, Halloween, it's time
to play rebel commander.
How else can I see the world
If I'm always stuck in this bomb shelter
of a bedroom?
The snow is determined tonight,
flexing its bustle
and I wonder where I can

go to be seen, be a presence.
Feeling the air tickle my arm hair . . .
it's invigorating.
I meet Joey and Lindsay
at 7-11
And we high-five each other,
ready to eat all the candy
our stomachs can withstand.
Just as darkness envelops the city,
we hopskip our way to Vernon Street,
me looking all Star Wars
Lindsay in her Pokémon outfit
Joey in a hard hat and workman's belt.
His dad is in construction.
Joey isn't too imaginative.

So when the storm hits
we're bags deep in mini Twix
Jelly Belly boxes
fudge squares.
My smile is hurting my face.
Is this what fun feels like?
If so, I want to dunk my face in it,
like those old movies of kids bobbing for apples.
This is eons away from
quiet nights with Mom,
watching her sew
studying myself in the mirror
thinking, *Is this it?!*

Why do they treat me so like glass close to breaking?

## III.

The storm's rainwater slithers down the sidewalk,
forming slick rivers between our giddy feet.
We want nothing else but to keep trick 'n' speaking all night.
As sudden as a lightning crack,
I slip
the kind of fall that has you about to land face first, but you
quickly jab your palms out to catch your shame,
and I do.
When I look down, I expect to see
blood dotting the pavement,
running to my wrists,
but instead I see cotton darting from my skin,
strands now wet from the falling rain,
and I poke this cotton,
where blood should be.

Now tears are pooling under my body.
Lindsay and Joey are too stunned to speak,
to even help me up.
All they can see is a boy in the rain
his body made of stuffing,
just a cuddle thing for his widowed mother
who lost her husband to a car crash.
Wait, was I there too?

I have a scar on my forehead no one origin-storied,
and I don't need to sleep as long as other people,
and I'm picking cotton from my insides on this street
and I'm crying for the boy I once was,
for the doll I now am, always have been.

## Short Forms

HRU
Kewl
WTF you doing 2day?
LMAO
TTYL
BRB
JK
I'm here.
DYT. No? Do Your Thing.
FWIW NRN

# Exhibit

I don't know how he did this,
but the museum curator
displayed photos
of every fractured moment
within every relationship I've ever had.

My ex-girlfriends follow me around the exhibit,
like some side-eye Mona Lisas,
but now I'm imagining their thought bubbles hovering over each head:
*Wow, David, you have the audacity to show up here
and take stock of what we had?! Pssht.*

I can actually feel the spittle with each Pssht.

This catalogue of bony arguments and overcooked excuses
reminds me of how I've fallen,
dusted my knees, got back up,
only to stammer back down again.

Down each hallway
there's a tiny shame getting bigger in my chest
when I pass by Lydia, Alejandra, Rebecca . . .
What could've been.
What should've been.
But I remind myself
regrets are for those who self-flagellate
to give themselves holy battle scars.
And I've never been one to withstand pain.

# People to Avoid

The girl with the 24/7 eyes searching for any cracks in the pavement
to parade in front of your face for days.

The man with the flint for fingers, the smile a match,
the suit jacket a castaway still jonesing for its first shoulders.

The seller of wishes, with apocalyptic taglines, selfish breath.

The editor holstering the red pen in favour of a quick passage to 5pm.

The police officers whose faces grin en masse when they remember
the crunch of knuckles against midnight flesh.

The joyless seeking a cozy comfort when their grey spreads overcast on those
with sparkles in their eyelashes.

The addicts hugging you to only find a shortcut to get closer to your jeans'
pockets.

The kissers using tongues as crossbows.

The preachers who fling brimstones at the rainbow cakes, icing flying into
their ear canals, the only sweet they allow into their bodies.

The world builders who tell you how you should speak, write, play,
a burden they carry and want to offload on anyone near them.

The mirror makers who never turn the glass to their own faces.

## 'Til It's Gone

When it all went down,
it was like *The Handmaid's Tale* spooned
*Brave New World*
as Harlan Ellison's Ticktockman watched
in the corner
and licked greedy lips.

The cameras played mannequin;
all seeing, never showing their hands.
The infirm were sent to labour camps,
which made little sense.
But when you realized how fit men and women
were being conscripted to fight the Chinese . . .
Well. Some things clicked into place
with the kind of dread reserved for snuff films.

I'll never look at a noose the same way again.
I'll never smell burnt hair and not wretch
and shudder
and dig fingernails into palms.

We were the lucky ones.
We hid in my uncle's bunker,
and now I feel rainstorm about all those phone conversations
where he rambled on about his warnings,
his "inside man"
as our eyes rolled in unison.
Even saying his name randomly would have
us clutching our sides and grinning for hours.

Today, we follow every order,
find ways to scavenge for the larder he began,
head to bed before police crawl along our streets.

How can we thank him? We don't.
Because he knows this isn't the end.
The finale is staggering towards us
with zombie arms
and Frankenstein eyes.
The Internet is dead, they say.
I never thought I'd hear those words.

How can the entire network die?

I shouldn't be surprised, though.
So many things have died.
Not just my friends. But that tiny
voice in our chests that squeaked out
self-help quotes of sacrifice, redemption.

It's a lighter's gasping flick now.
Blue fame sputtering and wheezing.

How did that song go again?
Not knowing what you've got until it's gone.

# Unfold

### I.

In the shiny museum, we avoid looking at the reconstruction
        of the 21-st century body.
We turn our eyes to the ceiling,
a clutch of fake stars welcoming us.

### II.

When we get home, we unfold our bodies
        like suede suitcases,
all soft folds and deep sighs.
The museum forced us to remember how it used to be,
        how we could see the fracture in each other's faces.
We should have stayed home.

### III.

In the morning, we creak our screws into the sunlight
        tell ourselves we'll do something lightning today.
We've had enough of the rain. The soggy highways.
When we pass by a dog wandering by itself
        we both smile, we both admire his curious teeth.

## Mall Rats

There,
arching grey fingers into blue canopy
there
that spire of a mall abandoned
a coffin of mothball neglect
there
see that RadioShack sign,
covered in Gap receipts?
I used to go there
once upon a timeless.

That New York Fries skeleton,
see it?
I made some bad decisions
there
you can tell a lot about someone
by how they talk to their friends
you can feel the aura of a city
by its graveyard of shopping shrines,
now a future set for a copycat zombie movie
 on these floors,
you could still sniff our hunger
appetizing on the recycled air
clouding our linear thoughts.
We ate coloured popcorn, sweet Jebus!
we went derelict on comics stores
that betrothed us to D&D fan bases
like they were our first summer camp buddies

The mall bent over forward to cover
its parking lot pathway with rose petals,
insidious welcome.
Under its sugar, the come-hither finger
was greasy with the sweat of milking money
from enthusiastic wallets.
When did it all end for them?
how soon after the Crash
did the mewl of mega-fists rain
purple on our faces?

## Nature Algorithms

Foxes are just animals running cat software on dog hardware.

Mosquitoes are spam emails you keep swatting until your attention recoils and you just give in to the swarm.

Bees flail into windows, trying to escape this room, with all the panic of an Uber driver whose Waze suddenly bugged out.

Sharks bear down on prey with the grin of copyright lawyers salivating at YouTube uploads.

The endangered Philippine eagle looks around for his friends, like anyone who joined Google+.

Fire-red ants are revenge-porn sites. No one likes you. Delete account.

A giraffe's neck is infinite scroll.

A dog's lick, when you need it most, is the Wi-Fi signal resurfacing magically after tethering to your phone's data.

A turtle's slow march to the other side of the road is the progress bar of an upload inching towards 100% of what you want right now.

# Famous Works of Literature that Also Describe the Night I Made Out with My First Alien

Great Expectations

The Heart is a Lonely Hunter

Stranger in a Strange Land

Be Cool

Contact

Tender Is the Night

If This Isn't Nice, What Is?

Good Bones

Surfacing

Things Fall Apart

Something Wicked This Way Comes

As I Lay Dying

The Naked and the Dead

The Beast That Shouted Love at the Heart of the World

I Have No Mouth, But I Must Scream

And Then There Were None.

# The Ghosts that Love Me

They drift at will,
floating in and out of my walls,
quick to vanish when I stare too long.

I'm not sure when my dead friends started swaying
over my shoulder
but the dust swirled that first time
when Zac hovers above my bed,
a joint winking on his lips.
I almost crackle with laughter.
I almost reach out for a clap-hug.
Then he passes me the joint,
And my hand passes through his.

Marsha catches me in a snowstorm,
lobs transparent snowballs at my back,
all the while, she dances,
(god, she could move as smooth as seaweed in lakes)
she also cries,
still shimmying to no music,
and I'm reminded of how depression
flicked its embers on her hair,
lighting a fire she never wanted.
I dance with her, but I don't cry.
She always loved my smile.

Wane and wax,
the moon lanterns my walk home from the Jays game.
Hovering above me, Marli is frowning,
track marks dotting her neck.
I want to ask her if she's OK now,
but such a cliché question ferments in my gut.
I just want her close.
I'm tempted to call Jason,
let him know his sister is here,
a mile away from where they grew up,
as the moon languishes behind brewing clouds.
Marli meanders into a park. Looking back at me.
I don't follow her.

## For Emily

Close your eyes.
Picture a twin world,
one where you got papercuts on your neck
after burying your head so deep in books.
Paper books.

Hear the crackle of phone lines clearing their throat,
      the timbre of language finding their loudspeakers.

Feel the runaway breeze weave between hair follicles,
      revel in the grass blades waving high between your toes.
Let the nomadic clouds drift you
      away from the boxes of light designed to
distract, consume, meander.

So.

You might have heard this from your mother and father.
But.
Be a question mark in a ballroom of exclamation darts.

Be a toaster hug against frowning hearts.
Be dancing like everyone is watching.
Be silly putty in a catwalk of shiny hand-me-downs.

Find the local motive
to ferry you from flavour to flavour,
from danger to saviour,
if only to feel the carbonated blood
bubble under your skin
to let you know you have lived,
truly paradised,
in a Lego castle built to make you look and be just like everyone else.

You were born with the Internet
 as a third hand,
high-fiving you endlessly,
        this guide dog leading you to, well,
            anywhere.
You traipse into the reverse-chron pathways
of getting the latest updates framed by the flashbulbs of
BREAKING NEWS!
as if the mediascapes you inhabit want you to only slip
into the skin of today, and not just today, but to-this-second.
So sample the archive of eras long pushed from your feed's
swaggering mouth.
Find a Victorian costume party that knows no hashtag.
Get lost on a fall afternoon. Break your GPS.
Visit a patch of the city unknown to
Google Maps drive-thrus.
Slow-cook your way into an autobiography you'd be
            proud to call your own.

# Bookmobile

When I was a kid, Thursday was the day I anticipated most.

At school, I stared down the clock
until the bell sprung my legs to run home,
where I would engulf dinner, mumble one-word
answers to my parents' questions and . . . wait . . .
staring at my living room clock,
until 6 p.m. struck delight into my little nerdy body.
For it was then,
between 6 and 8
that I could enter the holiest of shrines
no synagogue could match:
The Bookmobile!

Nestled behind a Price Chopper
in a parking lot that was best known for covert beers
and joint circles
squatted a small van plainly marked
with Toronto Public Library logos
and a rainbow that had seen better paint.
Three small steps led up to the machine's guts
where book spines gave me the backbone to dive deep
into waters I never wanted to leave.

I pulled down Tolkien classics
Piers Anthony fantasy
Ray Bradbury stories
X-Men comics
Clive Barker monsters
Salman Rushdie magic

The Bookmobile tumbled fiction into my throat
like a desert nomad keg-standing a water fountain.

It was here I felt among my people.
And by my people I mean
the grey-haired ladies debating
which Timothy Findley
to take out for a night on the couch
the wiry single men piling their bags high
with Asimov
the parents ushering their kids
into a playground of MAD Magazines.

And we all smiled at each other, but rarely spoke,
except for the whispery "excuse me" when our bodies huddled too close
together over the same shelf.
We didn't need to pretend to be social.

While others my age salivated at the idea of Saturday night hockey on CBC
Thursday night had me feeling
like a don, cherry-picking my allies in the fight against boredom.
I remember an English class too heavy with droning teacher voice.
I had to escape into the footnote glory of Tolkien's Silmarillion
but the teacher flagged my downward gaze,
penalized me with detention,
which gave me another hour of reading glory, huzzah!
My parents couldn't help but laugh
at the irony of being punished
in English class for reading literature,
but that's the challenge of being bookcore for life:
your nerdery may be respected but not always appreciated.

It was different in the Bookmobile.
I felt safe there, even if sometimes I had
dangerous ideas,
like wanting to steal the van of books
and drive to a sunlit valley
so I could wallow in dozens of tomes
covered in paper cuts
dog-earing every page I wanted to revisit,
even if only to embrace the language of imagination.

Joseph Brodsky once said:
"There are worse crimes than burning books.
One of them is not reading them."

Whenever I catch Thursday rolling into 6 p.m.
my hand twitches toward my wallet, my library card,
like smokers nic'ing hard when they watch Mad Men.

Some addictions I never want to quit.

# Sense-ual

When we lost our sight in
The Great Flash
our other senses heightened
into skyscraper eyes.

Skin sifted under palms,
eyelids fluttered beside lips,
we could smell our feastings.
The remix of relationships
began when we learned
to see without seeing.

Some of us cowered
behind shadows of doubt.
Some of us allowed other fingers
to grace our curves.
It wasn't easy.
Nothing could have been smooth
at moments like when kids wept at
a sun they couldn't enjoy
hunting for the cement hands
they had to grope to find.

The Great Flash stole one power
but animated in us another.

It was a strange homecoming for
sensuality
but lovers grew,
and grew closer.
When lips massaged along stomachs, ribs,
a collective gasp seeped from open windows.
The night air took it all, filtered it,
and rearranged the collage into a beat
we could hear and memorize into our marrow.

## Listicle

ODDEST THING I SAID TO HER:
I can talk dirty in Hebrew, if you want, because you said Hebrew was kind of sexy to you, and, er, never mind.

GREATEST THING SHE SAID TO ME:
Your mouth belongs on my neck, Dave.

TRUEST STATEMENT I'VE EVER SAID:
There aren't enough cashews in this trail mix. But I'm with you, so I'm good.

MOST SURPRISING HEADBUTT:
When we broke from a kiss, breathless and trembling, and we both went down to go down on each other. Oh, the giggles.

MOST IMPULSIVE AFTERNOON:
When we made love in the cemetery, our noses flush with the danger of it all, the creepiness of the fall.

WORST PHONE CALL:
When you told me you were pregnant, I was on Dundas heading to Yonge, the soundtrack of downtown buzz getting louder than my tinnitus, and your question lumped my throat, smacked my larynx, forced two rotting words out of my mouth: "We can't."

QUIETEST NIGHT:
When I kept calling your name and you weren't there.

# Give Me

Give me those connected toasters
that double as Bluetooth speakers.

Give me the RFID Candy
telling me just exactly which horse hoof
took a trip into the gelatin parade.

Give me the Instagram Goggles
letting me blink once for a Like,
twice for an emoji-only comment.

Give me Hologram 2PAC
dipping Hologram Sharon Jones
who's singing a song from a Nano Prince.

Give me Next-Gen Bread Ties
so they'll stop house-partying in the corners of my kitchen floor.

Give me Small Pharma to bring down Big Pharma
to at least Medium Pharma.

Give me a Slack channel
dedicated to
emotional-intelligence memes.

Give me that keyboard triple-double
that #tbt fever
that live-tweeting hangover.

Give me the taste of metal. It feels so . . . now.

# The Gun

When we found Chekhov's gun,
Buried under a church in
Badenweiler, Germany,
Where he died,
We looked at each other's faces,
Like we wanted a neon sign
To point us the right way.

It was pointless.

We had the map to guide us to the gun,
The money from the New Literary Institute
To bring back these relics,
But an itch crawled under our fingernails,
Urging us to abandon our mission.

We had to talk the next day,
Thanks to a heavy sleep that
Shuttled us into dreams of glittering parades
And wives with lipstick fervor.

We hung Chekhov's gun on the mantle
At our rental apartment, in view of everyone
Sleeping snug in our mobile pods.

But . . .
      We should've read the books,
        Listened to the warning shots.
Chekhov's gun has to finds its way into palms
If it squints into daylight.

That's just the way it is.

The Institute told us the Old Rules still applied today.
We nodded, telling ourselves some tales
Just didn't stop wagging.

That was then.
Now, I'm the last one alive,
A living room splattered with blood, shells,
The tendrils of gunsmoke still curling in the air.

Chekhov's gun on the floor,
My head in my hands,
A refrain buzzing between my ears:

It's wrong to make promises you don't mean to keep.

## For My Mother

You're 90 and still
sending me VR messages
about lettuce recalls.
It's cute.

Why I'm saving this
letter for now,
I can't answer that in full.
I'm still sorting it out.
It's been a long time coming.

I never told you this before,
But when you leaned into reading,
I played copycat and purred and found those pages
to snug me to sleep,
and books inspired me to slide a pen into my hand
at 15
        and write with the abandon
        of someone who knew this was not
going to be just a hobby.
That was horizon gold to me
finding the recipe I never wanted to
leave my stomach.

I always considered myself an
extroverted introvert
because I got my extro from you
my intro from Dad,
one swimming to the surface over the
other
        on any given hour.

Your ease
at being an open palm
       pleas for help
goaded me to do the same,
despite the selfish hat I pulled down
over my eyes,
wishing away other narrators
who had a story to tell about me.

This social lounging you displayed
—free of pander, a sly pinprick—
sighed its way into my everyday.
Quick, effortless,
like I'm truly my mother's son.
Like I'm the ringleader who knows everyone's
name
before they even sit down.

But. More than anything,
you taught me to keep smiling,
which has always been mayonnaise for me:
all day, on everything.

You never hustled me down a road
bubbling with the asphalt too hot for me to tread.
It was like you knew what to prescribe me:
matzo ball soup
and fuzzy blankets
John Irving books
told me I'd be alright, it just takes time to heal,
to shore that strength needed to fight
against the heat-haze designed to tire your bones,
to dull your resolve.

When I left the regatta,
>    won the race to
>    sample the downtown
grit,
your hugs didn't waver. Despite the miles between us.

I just don't say what I'm feeling all the time.
I know. Strange for a poet to admit.
Then again,
we can use the stage and page as open-heart therapy
when the dinner table becomes a melting pot
of surface talk.

Now, with your crow's feet dancing happily
to the Wii Aquafit you enjoy every night,
I want another quilt to keep your feet warm
when the chill comes in like a bad dream.

You have made me a man
I'm proud to admire in any given mirror.

There are nights when I appreciate in all that is holy that
I've bumped knuckles with the moonlight
under your roof,
your glow,
a gurgling paradise of brooks and fisher villages
sending me swift along its current,
>    always smiling.
>    tears waving high from my eyes.

## Villains

*One, two, Freddy's coming for you.*
*Three, four, better lock your door.*
*Five, six, grab your crucifix.*
*Seven, eight, gonna stay up late.*
*Nine, ten, never sleep*
*AGAIN!*

I'm watching horror movies for self-help tips.

It started with Freddy Krueger. And these days,
I can't really meet a Freddy without thinking of
a red-and-black checkered shirt
and cringe killphrases such as
"How sweet, fresh meat!"

The jokes stabbed me so quickly I barely noticed any blood.
I was smirking at Freddy's hypercolour punchlines
just silly nightmares I could flick away, no harm.
Krueger didn't keep me up at night
but instead taught me to grasp the humour in everything,
in tragedy
in pain
in the darkness that gift-wraps our dreams every night.

And that was only the beginning.

Because Jason taught me the stoic stealth of silent determination.
Carrie bled the blood of a daughter who
finally saw how wrong her mom could be.
The Shining told me, yeah, all work and no play makes everyone dull.
And with The Ring I realized kids in wells are creepy as fuck.

I go to zombie movie marathons at bars,
Order a coke and Romero, RIP George.
I pour out my liquor for a Nostradamus
who saw how we'd get turned without ever getting bit.

These days, I'm going through the back catalogue
like a hipster hunkers down with Dan Savage.
Chucky tells me I'm never too small to make a difference.
Pinhead scrubs the vanilla out of me so I get a bit more Neapolitan.
The Lost Boys remind me we all need to let loose once in awhile.
Michael Myers gives me a good reason to never hold grudges.

It's not just the slashers I'm watching for advice.
Every wide-eyed victim billboards the bravery of the foolish,
a new angle of admirable.
They got moxy, as my grandfather would say.
Thing is, they just suck at escaping.
Which we all do sometimes.

Then there's the MacGyver-loving
plucky and oh so lucky hero.
They trip the monster with piano wire
way before Home Alone did it.
They got DIY flamethrowers
chainsaws for hands
perfect aim in torrential rain.
It's all so shiny-happy
so rah-rah-sis-boom-bah.

But I gave up on horror's believability like
Mulder gave up on making a move on Scully in Season 1:
it's the anticipation of what could be that tickles the veins so deeply.

So give me the battle-cry screams,
and then the eyes dilated with courage.
This is what gives me hope that anyone can be a
Boomstick among twigs.
#EvilDead
#knowyourhorror

You might think it's oddball to find inspiration
in jump scares and monsters with bloody hockey masks.
Thing is, horror isn't designed to create fear—
it's meant to release it.
And I can do much more without fear.
      We all can.

## Today Is OK

I get the urge
To wander aimlessly in my own city
    All breathless eyes
And tapping feet

The Second Cup dispensaries finger-curling me
As a beacon beckon,
But I'm quick to tunnel-vision my pace,
Reveling in the quieter moments colouring my streets:
    The boy who puts down his phone to teach his
    Sister how to properly pet a dog.
    The kite, yes, a goddamn kite,
    Pirouetting against the blue of day.
    The two women clasping hands against
    The fight they consistently hold in their marrow.

I'm in High Park now, it's not how it used to be,
But that's the way it is, today is OK,
And the gilded walkways with robo-shuttles
Fade from my periphery.
I'm focused on seeing the small fireworks
crinkle around this green escape,
    This peppermint latte mist
The smiles and nods from others
Remind me we're in this together,
Whatever we decide "this" truly is,
And if we don't agree then we can just
    Do as the birds do,
    And chirp our simple joys
    And simpler pains
    As if we could summon a sudden urge to just fly,
    Careen out of here, like our life depends on it.
    Maybe it does.

# When They Killed the Journalists

When they killed the journalists
we saw patches for the "DIY or Die" tattoo
on the tablet bags of kids with spiked hair
and eyebrow studs.
Hackles raised, fists balled,
these were the new citizen journalists
who replaced the template of decades past,
who even supplanted the citizen media
of the early 2000s.

It's not like our news climate had a choice,
as the overflowing sun germinated
a new kind of heat poring our foreheads.
After all, after it all, the laptops stopped scrolling
we didn't have enough journalism to give way to page
after page
after page.

These citizens turned journalists just had to report on
the basic anatomy of the spineless leaders pointing fingers
at "the enemy of the people"
the archives got vaulted by blindfolded paperwork
the speeches never invited anyone but paid supporters
to clap breathlessly for every sculpted statement.

| David Silverberg

# When We Die

We don't get the book of life
like Hebrew day school taught us.

Instead, our hands are filled with a generous tome
bound by the leaves we tumbled into as kids
and flipping through each page,
we see how this isn't what we expected at all
and our breath cramps in our throat as we realize
this is a "Choose Your Own Adventure"
where all the decisions made are inscribed
in a luminescent calligraphy
punctuated by the outcomes that could've
been. If only.

Can we hurdle the regret bouldering
inside our dead throats?
Does it matter if we do, now?

# The End of It All

I have too many dreams
about the end of it all.
The glaciers harpooning into coastal cities
nuclear-armed Gideons raining spears
on our upturned heads.

I chew my food slowly—for once—
to let the flavour linger on my palate.
Who knows when I'll have this cheesecake again?

I wake up with drenched pillows
my sheets snaking over my legs,
the peeking sunlight shocking my eyelids.

I feel so silly waking up,
my thoughts now entrenched in the mundane.
Like where I can buy those
brown shoelaces for my dress shoes
or how I can leap over the New York Times paywall.

I should be building
a bomb shelter filled with
essentials.
Harlan Ellison books.
Canned mushroom soup.
Jenga. And where can I get a laptop battery pack?

My friends poke me in the ribs
when I tell them about the dreams.
They don't get it.
Few people do.
They don't know how dangerous
this storm has become.
The wax figures are melting.
The espresso machines are fighting their owners.

David Silverberg

Everyone is laughing way too hard—it's not natural.

But me, I keep having these dreams about
a future seething with a brimstone valley,
trees looking like matchsticks about to burn your fingers.

I should stop watching apocalypse movies, my mom says.
I should stop dreaming, I tell myself. As if that ever works.
Instead, I hide under covers until afternoon creaks wide,
eyelashes a grateful moth,
cats mewling for food.
If the world ends with a whisper,
I'll be ready to wallow in its sweet everything.

# Acknowledgements

I have so many people to thank, because I'm graced by the love and support of dozens of wonderful friends and family. I first want to thank my family—Mom, Dad, Ben, Karen and Emily—and my extended family for always being there for me. The entire Toronto Poetry Slam community deserves some love, from the members of the Toronto Poetry Project collective to everyone who is part of this incredible slamily (I'm sorry, I couldn't resist).

Then there are my supportive friends from back in the day—you know who you are.

Finally, thank you to my editor Sandra for believing in me with this new poetry collection. Her wisdom and insight on fine-tuning the first draft taught me a lot about where I can go with my poetry.

## About the Author

David Silverberg is a poet, journalist, editor, and event producer. He founded Toronto Poetry Slam, one of the most popular poetry events in Canada. He's the editor of the Canadian spoken word anthology *Mic Check* (Quattro Books). David's non-fiction work has appeared in *The Washington Post, BBC News, Vice, Descant,* and *The Globe & Mail.* His first solo show, *Jewnique,* debuted in 2018.
Find him at www.davidsilverberg.ca.